Uncommon Prayer? Use of 1662

-

The Order for
Holy Communion,
or **Mass**
as commonly celebrated
after the form of the
1662
Book of Common Prayer

Demi-Horse Books™
2010

First issued March 2010

demiHorse Books™
34 Gledhow Wood Road, Leeds,
LS8 4BZ, UK

Copyright © Alec McGuire, 2010

The right of Alec McGuire to be identified as author of this work has been asserted by him in accordance with Section 77 of the Copyright, Designs and Patents Act 1988.

All rights reserved. No part of this publication may be reproduced, stored in a retrieval system, or transmitted, in any form or by any means, electronic, mechanical, photocopying, recording, or otherwise, without the prior permission of the publisher.

This book is sold subject to the condition that it shall not, by way of trade or otherwise, be lent, re-sold, hired out, or otherwise circulated without the publisher's prior consent in any form of binding or cover other than that in which it is published and without a similar condition including this condition being imposed on the subsequent purchaser.

ISBN: 978-0-9561560-3-7

CONTENTS

p5   Introduction;

p7   The Order for the HOLY COMMUNION, also known as The Mass, The Eucharist, and The Lord's Supper: after the Order of 1662 as commonly used;

p25   Collects for use with the Collect for the Day;

p29   The Proper Prefaces;

p31   Material sometimes used from the Order of 1549;

p35   Material sometimes used from the Order of 1928;

p41   Before and after the liturgy

p47   From the music of John Merbecke;

p51   A brief Commentary on Cranmer's liturgy;

INTRODUCTION

The Book of Common Prayer (BCP) contains services of uncommonly beautiful language, and extraordinarily inventive liturgical structure (of which more is said in the Commentary). Mattins and Evensong can easily be followed from a published copy of the BCP. It is otherwise with the Communion: the order printed in the BCP and the service performed in Church are so different that it is next to impossible for a newcomer to the service to follow it using a published BCP.

Some parts are no longer used at all; some are replaced by other texts; the rubrics do not describe what is actually done; and no account is taken in the BCP of hymns or other music. Publication of the Prayer Book is governed by Crown privilege, and only the version authorised by The Act of Uniformity can be published as a book. That doesn't prevent there being a need for a printed version that corresponds with the service as performed; and the "fair use" principle is generally understood to permit reproduction of limited portions of a text.

Things are complicated by the fact that different parishes and priests perform the service in varying ways (when they perform it at all); the variations have much to do with churchmanship – Low, Broad, High, Anglo-Catholic, etc. Some variations are less common and can be relegated to separate sections, marked 1549 and 1928. For the Ten Commandments, it is the case that there are no fewer than seven possibilities in wide(-ish) use; so I have included them all, in declining order of frequency. While I have allowed for a very wide range of variations, I have excluded those of *The English Missal*, at least where they lead to results that are hardly recognisable as the Prayer Book. Otherwise, in most Churches, the text presented in the main part of this little book should enable a newcomer to follow the service and save the experienced from flipping through unused pages.

A (partial) version of the music of Merbecke is added in a separate section. This is a modern transcription, by the author, of Merbecke's unharmonised original. What is sung in churches is usually a harmonised arrangement with Merbecke's rhythms smoothed out. However, Merbecke's importance is such that it seemed important not to omit his music, and to indicate what he actually left us.

I have perforce had to rewrite the rubrics substantially, but hope that they are still in an appropriate style of language.

At the end, I have added a short commentary on the history of 1662 and its use, and, perhaps more importantly, on why it has the structure it has. Cranmer did not make a mistake in setting out the precursor rite, 1552, as he did; in fact, he produced a work of liturgical genius that no form of service in the reformed tradition has ever come close to equalling.

It is 461 years since Cranmer's First Book appeared; may his work still be used in the year 2471 (if the human race, Christianity in the western world, and the Anglican tradition themselves still exist, of course...).

Alec McGuire
March 2010

The 1662 Order as commonly used

INTRODUCTORY LITURGY

As the Celebrant Priest and other Clergy and ministers enter, an hymn may be sung and the Altar may be incensed.

The Priest, standing at the side of the Altar, says the Lord's Prayer alone, the people kneeling.

Our Father, which art in heaven, Hallowed be thy name, Thy kingdom come, Thy will be done, In earth as it is in heaven. Give us this day our daily bread. And forgive us our trespasses, As we forgive them that trespass against us; And lead us not into temptation, But deliver us from evil. Amen.

And then this Collect, the people answering, Amen.

Almighty God, unto whom all hearts be open, all desires known, and from whom no secrets are hid: Cleanse the thoughts of our hearts by the inspiration of thy Holy Spirit, that we may perfectly love thee, and worthily magnify thy holy Name; through Christ our Lord. **Amen.**

Then the Priest, turning him to the people, shall say one of the forms following, and the people, still kneeling, shall answer as shown and thereby ask God's mercy and grace.
The First Form is most customarily used, but the others at the Priest's discretion or according to the season.

First Form

First Form: **OUR LORD'S SUMMARY OF THE LAW**
Priest: Our Lord Jesus Christ said: Hear O Israel, the Lord thy God is one Lord, and thou shalt love the Lord thy God with all thy heart and with all thy soul and with all thy mind and with all thy strength. This is the first and great commandment, and the second is like, namely this: Thou shalt love thy neighbour as thyself. There is none other commandment greater than these. On these two commandments hang all the law and the prophets.
People: **Lord, have mercy upon us, and write these laws in our hearts, we beseech thee.** *or:* **Lord, have mercy upon us, and write all these thy laws in our hearts, we (humbly) beseech thee.**
(continued page 11)

Second Form: **Kyries**
Priest: Lord, have mercy upon us.
People: **Christ, have mercy upon us.**
Priest: Lord, have mercy upon us.

Third Form
Priest: Lord, have mercy. *People:* **Lord, have mercy.**
Priest: Christ, have mercy *People*: **Christ, have mercy.**
Priest: Lord, have mercy. *People:* **Lord, have mercy.**

*Fourth Form**
Priest: Lord, have mercy. *People:* **Lord, have mercy.**
Priest: Lord, have mercy. *People:* **Christ, have mercy.**
Priest: Christ, have mercy. *People:* **Christ, have mercy.**
Priest: Lord, have mercy. *People:* **Lord, have mercy.**
Priest: Lord, have mercy.

*: *The difference between the third and fourth forms can be recognised by the Priest's second sentence.*

Fifth and Sixth Forms:
As for the third and fourth forms, but using the phrases: Kyrie eleison, Christe eleison, Kyrie eleison.

Seventh Form: **THE TEN COMMANDMENTS**
Priest: God spake these words, and said: I am the Lord thy God: Thou shalt have none other Gods but me.
People: **Lord, have mercy upon us, and incline our hearts to keep this law.**
Thou shalt not make to thyself any graven image, nor the likeness of any thing that is in heaven above, or in the earth beneath, or in the water under the earth. Thou shalt not bow down to them, nor worship them. For I the Lord your God am a jealous God, and visit the sins of the fathers upon the children unto the third and fourth generation of them that hate me, and shew mercy unto thousands in them that love me and keep my commandments.
Lord, have mercy upon us, and incline our hearts to keep this law.
Thou shalt not take the Name of the Lord thy God in vain: for the Lord will not hold him guiltless, that taketh his Name in vain.
Lord, have mercy upon us, and incline our hearts to keep this law.
Remember that thou keep holy the Sabbath day. Six days shalt thou labour, and do all that thou hast to do; but the seventh day is the Sabbath of the Lord thy God. In it thou shalt do no manner of work, thou, and thy son, and thy daughter, thy man-servant, and thy maid-servant, thy cattle, and the stranger that is within thy gates. For in six days the Lord made heaven and earth, the sea, and all that in them is, and rested the seventh

day: wherefore the Lord blessed the seventh day, and hallowed it.

Lord, have mercy upon us, and incline our hearts to keep this law.

Honour thy father and thy mother; that thy days may be long in the land which the Lord thy God giveth thee.

Lord, have mercy upon us, and incline our hearts to keep this law.

Thou shalt do no murder.

Lord, have mercy upon us, and incline our hearts to keep this law.

Thou shalt not commit adultery.

Lord, have mercy upon us, and incline our hearts to keep this law.

Thou shalt not steal.

Lord, have mercy upon us, and incline our hearts to keep this law.

Thou shalt not bear false witness against thy neighbour.

Lord, have mercy upon us, and incline our hearts to keep this law.

Thou shalt not covet thy neighbour's house, thou shalt not covet thy neighbour's wife, nor his servant, nor his maid, nor his ox, nor his ass, nor any thing that is his.

Lord, have mercy upon us, and write all these thy laws in our hearts, we beseech thee.

LITURGY OF THE WORD

Then the Priest, standing as before, shall say the **COLLECT** *appointed for the day, and any others chosen (see p22), the people distinctly answering* **Amen** *to each one.*

Immediately after the Collects, the **EPISTLE** *shall be read, the people seated. The Minister that readeth the Epistle shall say,* THE EPISTLE [*or:* THE PORTION OF SCRIPTURE APPOINTED FOR THE EPISTLE] IS WRITTEN IN THE ------ CHAPTER OF -------- BEGINNING AT THE ------- VERSE. *And the Epistle ended, the Epistoller shall say:* HERE ENDETH THE EPISTLE.

Then an hymn or psalm may be sung. The Priest shall go to the mid-point of the Altar.

Then shall be read the **GOSPEL** *(the people all standing up, and all turning to face the reading), the Gospeller saying,* THE HOLY GOSPEL IS WRITTEN IN THE ----- CHAPTER OF ----- BEGINNING AT THE ----- VERSE.
And the people may respond to this announcement, **Glory be to thee, O Lord.**
And the Gospel ended, the people may say: **Praise be to thee, O Christ.**
At the Gospel, incense may be used.

And then there shall be said

And then there shall be said or sung the **CREED** *following, the people still standing as before, but facing East.*

I believe in one God **the Father Almighty, Maker of heaven and earth, And of all things visible and invisible.**

And in one Lord *(here bow)* ***Jesus Christ,*** the only-begotten Son of God, Begotten of his Father before all worlds, God of God, Light of Light, Very God of very God, Begotten, not made, Being of one substance with the Father, By whom all things were made: Who for us men, and for our salvation came down from heaven, *(here genuflect)* ***And was incarnate by the Holy Ghost of the Virgin Mary, And was made man,*** And was crucified also for us under Pontius Pilate. He suffered and was buried, And the third day he rose again according to the scriptures, And ascended into heaven, And sitteth on the right hand of the Father. And he shall come again with glory to judge both the quick and the dead: Whose kingdom shall have no end.

And I believe in the Holy Ghost, The Lord and giver of life, Who proceedeth from the Father and the Son, Who with the Father and the Son together *(here bow)* ***is worshipped*** and glorified, Who spake by the Prophets.

And I believe one (holy) Catholick and Apostolick Church. I acknowledge one Baptism for the remission of sins. And I look for the Resurrection of the dead, And the life ✠ of the world to come. Amen.

Then shall follow the **SERMON** *if any, as also Banns of Matrimony may be published and notices given.*

LITURGY OF THE EUCHARIST

Then shall the Priest begin the **OFFERTORY**, *saying this or one or more other prescribed sentences, as he thinketh most convenient in his discretion.*

Let your light so shine before men, that they may see your good works, and glorify your Father which is in heaven.

Then an hymn may be sung; and the alms of the people be received and reverently brought to the Priest, who shall humbly present them at the Holy Table.
And the Priest shall place upon the Altar so much Bread and Wine, as he shall think sufficient. And the oblations and the Altar may be incensed, as signifying the prayers of the ministers and people.

THE EUCHARISTIC PRAYER OR CANON

After which done, and the people kneeling, the Priest shall say:

Let us pray for the whole state of Christ's Church militant here in earth.

ALMIGHTY and everliving God, who by thy holy Apostle hast taught us to make prayers and supplications, and to give thanks, for all men: We humbly beseech thee most mercifully to accept our alms and oblations, and to receive these our prayers, which we offer unto thy Divine Majesty; beseeching thee to inspire continually the universal Church with the spirit of truth, unity and concord: And grant, that all they that do confess thy holy name may agree in the truth of thy holy Word, and live in unity and godly love.

We beseech thee also to save and defend all Christian Kings, Princes, and Governors; and specially thy servant *ELIZABETH* our Queen; that under her we may be godly and quietly governed. And grant unto her whole Council, and to all that are put in authority under her, that they may truly and indifferently minister justice, to the punishment of wickedness and vice, and to the maintenance of thy true religion, and virtue.

Give grace, O heavenly Father, to all Bishops and Curates, that they may both by their life and doctrine set forth thy true and lively Word, and rightly and duly administer thy holy Sacraments: And to all thy people give thy heavenly grace; and specially to this congregation here present, that, with meek heart and due reverence, they may hear, and receive thy holy Word; truly serving thee in holiness and righteousness all the days of their life.

And we most humbly beseech thee of thy goodness, O Lord, to comfort and succour all them, who in this transitory life are in trouble, sorrow, need, sickness, or any other adversity.

And we also bless thy holy Name for all thy servants departed this life in thy faith and fear; beseeching thee to give us grace so to follow their good examples, that with them we may be partakers of thy heavenly kingdom:

Grant this, O Father, for Jesus Christ's sake, our only Mediator and Advocate. **Amen.**

Then shall the Priest say to them that come to receive the Holy Communion,

YE that do truly and earnestly repent you of your sins, and are in love and charity with your neighbours, and intend to lead a new life, following the commandments of God, and walking from henceforth in his holy ways:

DRAW near with faith, and take this Holy Sacrament to your comfort: and make your humble confession to Almighty God, meekly kneeling upon your knees.

Then shall this general **CONFESSION** *be made, in the name of all those that are minded to receive the Holy Communion, led by one of the Ministers, both he and all the people kneeling humbly upon their knees and saying,*

ALMIGHTY God, Father of our Lord Jesus Christ, Maker of all things, Judge of all men: We acknowledge and bewail our manifold sins and wickedness, Which we from time to time most grievously have committed, By thought, word, and

deed, Against thy Divine Majesty, Provoking most justly thy wrath and indignation against us. We do earnestly repent, And are heartily sorry for these our misdoings; The remembrance of them is grievous unto us; The burden of them is intolerable. Have mercy upon us, Have mercy upon us, most merciful Father; For thy Son our Lord Jesus Christ's sake, Forgive us all that is past; And grant that we may ever hereafter Serve and please thee In newness of life, To the honour and glory of thy Name; Through Jesus Christ our Lord. Amen.

Then shall the Priest (or the Bishop, being present,) stand up, and turning himself to the people, pronounce this **ABSOLUTION**.

A LMIGHTY God, our heavenly Father, who of his great mercy hath promised forgiveness of sins to all them that with hearty repentance and true faith turn unto him: Have mercy upon you; Pardon ✠ and deliver you from all your sins; confirm and strengthen you in all goodness; and bring you to everlasting life; through Jesus Christ our Lord. **Amen.**

¶ *Then shall the Priest say,*

Hear what comfortable words our Saviour Christ saith unto all that truly turn to him.
Come unto me all that travail and are heavy laden, and I will refresh you.
St Matthew 11.28
So God loved the world, that he gave his only-begotten Son, to the end that all that believe in him should not perish, but have everlasting life.
St John 3.16

Hear also what Saint Paul saith.
This is a true saying, and worthy of all men to be received, that Christ Jesus came into the world to save sinners.

1 Timothy 1.15

Hear also what Saint John saith.
If any man sin, we have an Advocate with the Father, Jesus Christ the righteous; and he is the propitiation for our sins.

1 St John 2.1

After which, the people all standing up, the Priest shall proceed, saying,

(Priest:	The Lord be with you.
Answer:	**And with thy spirit.)**
Priest:	Lift up your hearts.
Answer:	**We lift them up unto the Lord.**
Priest:	Let us give thanks unto our Lord God.
Answer:	**It is meet and right so to do.**

Then shall the Priest turn to the Altar, and say,

It is very meet, right, and our bounden duty, that we should at all times, and in all places, give thanks unto thee, O Lord, *Holy Father, Almighty, Everlasting God.

*These words [Holy Father] must be omitted on Trinity Sunday.

Here shall follow the Proper Preface, according to the time, if there be any specially appointed (p29): or else immediately shall follow:

Therefore with Angels and Archangels and with all the company of heaven, we laud and magnify thy glorious name: evermore praising thee, and saying,

Holy, holy, holy

Holy, holy, holy, Lord God of hosts, heaven and earth are full of thy glory. ℣ Glory be to thee, O Lord most High. Amen. ℣ (℣...℣ or Hosanna in the highest.)
{*This anthem may be added:* **Blessed ✠ is he that cometh in the name of the Lord. Hosanna in the highest.**}

Then shall the Priest, kneeling down at the Altar, say in the name of all them that shall receive the Communion this Prayer (of **HUMBLE ACCESS**) *following (they kneeling and joining with him),*

WE do not presume to come to this thy Table, O merciful Lord, trusting in our own righteousness, but in thy manifold and great mercies. We are not worthy so much as to gather up the crumbs under thy Table. But thou art the same Lord, whose property is always to have mercy: Grant us therefore, gracious Lord, so to eat the flesh of thy dear Son Jesus Christ, and to drink his blood, that our sinful bodies may be made clean by his body, and our souls washed through his most precious blood, and that we may evermore dwell in him, and he in us. Amen.

When the Priest, standing before the Altar, hath so ordered the Bread and Wine, that he may with the more readiness and decency break the Bread and take the Cup into his hands, he shall say the Prayer of Consecration as followeth.

ALMIGHTY God, our heavenly Father, who of thy tender mercy didst give thine only Son Jesus Christ to suffer death upon the Cross for our redemption, who made there (by his one oblation of himself once offered) a full, perfect, and sufficient sacrifice, oblation, and satisfaction, for the sins of the whole world; and did institute, and in his holy Gospel command us to continue, a perpetual memory of that his precious death, until his coming again:

Hear§ us, O merciful Father, we most humbly beseech thee; and grant that we receiving these thy creatures of ✠ bread and ✠ wine, according to thy Son our Saviour Jesus Christ's holy institution, in remembrance of his death and passion, may be partakers of his most blessed ✠ Body and ✠ Blood: who in the same night that he was betrayed, ᵃtook Bread; and when he had given ✠ thanks, ᵇhe brake it, and gave it to his disciples, saying, Take, eat; ᶜTHIS IS MY BODY WHICH IS GIVEN FOR YOU: Do this in remembrance of me. Likewise after supper ᵈhe took the Cup; and when he had given ✠ thanks, he gave it to them saying, Drink ye all of this; ᵉfor THIS IS MY BLOOD OF THE NEW TESTAMENT, which is shed for you and for many for the remission of sins: Do this, as oft as ye shall drink it, in remembrance of me. **Amen.**

§ Here the Priest may raise his eyes, as if towards heaven;
✠ And here may make the sign of the Cross.
a: Here the Priest is to take the Paten into his hands:
b: And here to break the Bread:
c: And here to lay his hand upon all the Bread.
d: Here he is to take the Cup into his hands:
e: And here to lay his hand on every vessel (be it Chalice or Flagon) in which there is any wine to be consecrated.

(Then this Anthem may be used:
O LAMB OF GOD, THAT TAKEST AWAY THE SINS OF THE WORLD: HAVE MERCY UPON US (X2); GRANT US THY PEACE.*)*

Then shall the Priest

Then shall the Priest first receive the Communion in both kinds himself, and then proceed to deliver the same to the Bishops, Priests and Deacons, in like manner (if any be present), and after that to the people also, all meekly kneeling.

And when he delivereth the Bread to any one, he shall say,

The Body of our Lord Jesus Christ, which was given for thee, preserve thy body and soul unto everlasting life. ...

And the Minister that delivereth the Cup to any one shall say,

The Blood of our Lord Jesus Christ, which was shed for thee, preserve thy body and soul unto everlasting life. ...

Then, all having received the Communion, shall the Priest and people say the Lord's Prayer.

OUR Father **which art in heaven, Hallowed be thy name, Thy kingdom come, Thy will be done; In earth as it is in heaven. Give us this day our daily bread; And forgive us our trespasses, As we forgive them that trespass against us; And lead us not into temptation, But deliver us from evil. For thine is the kingdom, The power, and the glory, For ever and ever. Amen.**

After which the Priest shall continue and say as followeth:

O LORD and heavenly Father, we thy humble servants entirely desire thy fatherly goodness mercifully to accept this our sacrifice of praise and thanksgiving; most humbly beseeching thee to grant, that by the merits and death of thy Son Jesus Christ, and through faith in his blood, we and all thy whole Church may obtain remission of our sins, and all other benefits of his passion. And here we offer and present unto thee, O Lord, ourselves, our souls and bodies, to be a reasonable, holy, and lively sacrifice unto thee; humbly beseeching thee, that all we, who are partakers of this holy Communion, may be fulfilled with thy grace and heavenly benediction. And although we be unworthy, through our manifold sins, to offer unto thee any sacrifice, yet we beseech thee to accept this our bounden duty and service; not weighing our merits, but pardoning our offences, through Jesus Christ our Lord, by whom, and with whom, in the unity of the holy Ghost, all honour and glory be unto thee, O Father Almighty, world without end. **Amen.**

Or this:

ALMIGHTY and everliving God, we most heartily thank thee, for that thou dost vouchsafe to feed us, who have duly received these holy mysteries, with the spiritual food of the most precious Body and Blood of thy Son our Saviour Jesus Christ; and dost assure us thereby of thy favour and goodness towards us; and that we are very members incorporate in the mystical body of thy Son, which is the blessed company of all faithful people; and are also heirs through hope of thy everlasting kingdom, by the merits of the most precious death and passion of thy dear Son. And we most humbly beseech thee, O heavenly Father, so to assist us with thy grace, that we may continue in that holy fellowship, and do all such good works as thou hast prepared for us to walk in; through Jesus Christ our Lord, to whom with thee and the Holy Ghost, be all honour and glory, world without end. **Amen.**

(Here endeth the Eucharistic Prayer or Canon)

CONCLUDING LITURGY

Then shall be said or sung,

GLORY be to God on high, and in earth peace, good will towards men. We praise thee, we bless thee, *(here bow)* **we worship thee**, we glorify thee, we give thanks to thee for thy great glory, O Lord God, heavenly King, God the Father Almighty.

O Lord, the only-begotten Son, *(here bow)* **Jesu Christ;** O Lord God, Lamb of God, Son of the Father, that takest away the sins of the world, have mercy upon us. Thou that takest away the sins of the world, have mercy upon us. Thou that takest away the sins of the world, *(here bow)* **receive our prayer.** Thou that sittest at the right hand of God the Father, have mercy upon us.

For thou only art holy; thou only art the Lord; thou only, O Christ, with the Holy Ghost, art most high in the glory of God ✠ the Father. Amen.

Then the Priest (or Bishop if he be present) shall let them depart with this Blessing.

The peace of God, which passeth all understanding, keep your hearts and minds in the knowledge and love of God, and of his Son Jesus Christ our Lord: And the blessing of God Almighty, the Father, the Son, ✠ and the Holy Ghost, be amongst you and remain with you always. **Amen.**

In some churches, the Last Gospel (John 1.1-14) is said by the Priest at this point.

The Angelus (p42) is also sometimes said at this point.

As the Priest and Ministers leave an hymn may be sung.

COLLECTS
for use with the Collect for the Day

For the Sovereign

ALMIGHTY God, whose kingdom is everlasting, and power infinite: Have mercy upon the whole Church; and so rule the heart of thy chosen servant ELIZABETH, our Queen and Governor, that she (knowing whose minister she is) may above all things seek thy honour and glory: and that we and all her subjects (duly considering whose authority she hath) may faithfully serve, honour, and humbly obey her, in thee, and for thee, according to thy blessed Word and ordinance; through Jesus Christ our Lord, who with thee and the Holy Ghost liveth and reigneth, ever one God, world without end. **Amen.**

or:

ALMIGHTY and everlasting God, we are taught by thy holy Word, that the hearts of Kings are in thy rule and governance, and that thou dost dispose and turn them as it seemeth best to thy godly Wisdom: We humbly beseech thee so to dispose and govern the heart of ELIZABETH thy servant, our Queen and Governor, that in all her thoughts, words, and works, she may ever seek thy honour and glory, and study to preserve thy people committed to her charge, in wealth, peace, and godliness: Grant this, O merciful Father, for thy dear Son's sake, Jesus Christ our Lord. **Amen.**

For use at the discretion of the Minister.

ASSIST us mercifully, O Lord, in these our supplications and prayers, and dispose the way of thy servants towards the attainment of everlasting salvation; that, among all the changes and chances of this mortal life, they may ever be defended by thy most gracious and ready help; through Jesus Christ our Lord. **Amen.**

O ALMIGHTY Lord, and everlasting God, vouchsafe, we beseech thee, to direct, sanctify, and govern, both our hearts and bodies, in the ways of thy laws, and in the works of thy commandments; that through thy most mighty protection, both here and ever, we may be preserved in body and soul, through our Lord and Saviour Jesus Christ. **Amen.**

GRANT, we beseech thee, Almighty God, that the words, which we have heard this day with our outward ears, may through thy grace be so grafted inwardly in our hearts, that they may bring forth in us the fruit of good living, to the honour and praise of thy Name; through Jesus Christ our Lord. **Amen.**

PREVENT us, O Lord, in all our doings with thy most gracious favour, and further us with thy continual help; that in all our works, begun, continued, and ended in thee, we may glorify thy holy name, and finally by thy mercy obtain everlasting life; through Jesus Christ our Lord. **Amen.**

ALMIGHTY God, the fountain of all wisdom, who knowest our necessities before we ask, and our ignorance in asking: We beseech thee to have compassion upon our infirmities; and those things, which for our unworthiness we dare not, and for our blindness we cannot ask, vouchsafe to give us for the worthiness of thy Son Jesus Christ our Lord. **Amen.**

ALMIGHTY God, who hast promised to hear the petitions of them that ask in thy Son's Name: We beseech thee mercifully to incline thine ears unto us that have made now our prayers and supplications unto thee; and grant, that those things, which we have faithfully asked according to thy will, may effectually be obtained, to the relief of our necessity, and to the setting forth of thy glory; through Jesus Christ our Lord. **Amen.**

PROPER PREFACES

Upon Christmas Day, *and seven days after.*

BECAUSE thou didst give Jesus Christ thine only Son to be born as at this time for us; who, by the operation of the Holy Ghost, was made very man of the substance of the Virgin Mary his mother; and that without spot of sin, to make us clean from all sin. Therefore with Angels, *&c.*

Upon Easter Day, *and seven days after.*

BUT chiefly are we bound to praise thee for the glorious Resurrection of thy Son Jesus Christ our Lord: for he is the very Paschal Lamb, which was offered for us, and hath taken away the sin of the world; who by his death hath destroyed death, and by his rising to life again hath restored to us everlasting life. Therefore with Angels, *&c.*

Upon Ascension Day, *and seven days after.*

THROUGH thy most dearly beloved Son Jesus Christ our Lord; who after his most glorious Resurrection manifestly appeared to all his Apostles, and in their sight ascended up into heaven to prepare a place for us; that where he is, thither we might also ascend, and reign with him in glory. Therefore with Angels, *&c.*

Upon Whitsunday, *and six days after*

THROUGH Jesus Christ our Lord; according to whose most true promise, the Holy Ghost came down as at this time from heaven with a sudden great sound, as it had been a mighty wind, in the likeness of fiery tongues, lighting upon the Apostles, to teach them, and to lead them to all truth; giving them both the gift of divers languages, and also boldness with fervent zeal constantly to preach the Gospel unto all nations; whereby we have been brought out of darkness and error into the clear light and true knowledge of thee, and of thy Son Jesus Christ. Therefore with Angels, &c.

Upon the feast of Trinity *only.*
WHO art one God, one Lord; not one only Person, but three Persons in one Substance. For that which we believe of the glory of the Father, the same we believe of the Son, and of the Holy Ghost, without any difference or inequality. Therefore with Angels, &c.

Some 1549 Texts
which are occasionally used (spelling modernised)

after the Sanctus-Benedictus, part of the Canon proceeds as follows:

• • • O God, heavenly Father, which of thy tender mercy didst give thine only Son Jesus Christ to suffer death upon the Cross for our redemption, who made there (by his one oblation of himself once offered) a full, perfect, and sufficient sacrifice, oblation, and satisfaction, for the sins of the whole world, and did institute, and in his holy Gospel command us to celebrate, a perpetual memory of that his precious death, until his coming again:

Hear us (O merciful Father) we most humbly beseech thee; and with thy holy Spirit and word, vouchsafe to bl✠ess and sanc✠tify these thy gifts, and creatures of bread and wine, that they may be unto us the body and blood of thy most dearly beloved Son Jesus Christ, Who in the same night that he was betrayed: took Bread, and when he had blessed, and given thanks, he brake it, and gave it to his disciples, saying: Take, eat, THIS IS MY BODY WHICH IS GIVEN FOR YOU: Do this in remembrance of me. Likewise after supper he took the Cup; and when he had given thanks, he gave it to them saying: Drink ye all of this, for THIS IS MY BLOOD OF THE NEW TESTAMENT, which is shed for you and for many for remission of sins: Do this, as oft as ye shall drink it, in remembrance of me.

WHEREFORE O LORD and heavenly Father, according to the institution of thy dearly beloved son, our Saviour Jesu Christ, we thy humble servants do celebrate, and make here before thy divine Majesty, with these holy gifts, the memorial which thy Son hath willed us to make, having in remembrance his blessed passion, mighty resurrection, and glorious ascension, rendering unto thee most hearty thanks, for the innumerable benefits procured unto us by the same, entirely desiring thy fatherly goodness, mercifully to accept this our Sacrifice of praise and thanksgiving; most humbly beseeching thee to grant, that by the merits and death of the Son Jesus Christ, and through faith in his blood, we and all thy whole Church may obtain remission of our sins, and all other benefits of his passion. And here we offer and present unto thee (O Lord) ourselves, our souls, and bodies, to be a reasonable, holy, and lively sacrifice unto thee; humbly beseeching thee, that whosoever shall be partakers of this holy Communion, may worthily receive the most precious body and blood of thy Son Jesus Christ: and be fulfilled with thy grace and heavenly benediction, and made one body with thy son Jesu Christ, that he may dwell in them, and they in him. And although we be unworthy (through our manifold sins) to offer unto thee any sacrifice, yet we beseech thee to accept this our bounden duty and service, and command these our prayers and supplications, by the Ministry of thy holy Angels, to be brought up into thy holy Tabernacle before the sight of thy divine majesty; not weighing our merits, but pardoning our offences, through Christ our Lord, by whom, and with whom, in the unity of the holy Ghost:

all honour and glory be unto thee, O Father Almighty, world without end. **Amen.**

(if the above is used, the Lord's Prayer may be used before the communion, sometimes together with Prayer of Humble Access; even more rarely the Confession is moved to before the Communion)

After the Communion:

ALMIGHTY and everliving God, we most heartily thank thee, for that thou dost vouchsafe to feed us in these holy mysteries, with the spiritual food of the most precious Body and Blood of thy Son, our Saviour Jesus Christ, and hast assured us (duly receiving the same) of thy favour and goodness towards us, and that we are very members incorporate in thy Mystical body, which is the blessed company of all faithful people, and heirs through hope of thy everlasting kingdom, by the merits of the most precious death and passion of thy dear Son. We therefore most humbly beseech thee, O heavenly Father, so to assist us with thy grace, that we may continue in that holy fellowship, and do all such good works as thou hast prepared for us to walk in: through Jesus Christ our Lord, to whom with thee and the Holy Ghost, be all honour and glory, world without end. **Amen.**

Some 1928 Texts
which are occasionally used

Let us pray for the whole state of Christ's Church militant here in earth.

ALMIGHTY and everliving God, who by thy holy Apostle hast taught us to make prayers, and supplications, and to give thanks, for all men: We humbly beseech thee most mercifully to accept our alms and oblations, and to receive these our prayers, which we offer unto thy Divine Majesty; beseeching thee to inspire continually the universal Church with the spirit of truth, unity, and concord: And grant, that all they that do confess thy holy name may agree in the truth of thy holy Word, and live in unity and godly love.

We beseech thee also to lead all nations in the way of righteousness and peace; and so to direct all kings and rulers, that under them thy people may be godly and quietly governed. And grant unto thy servant *(ELIZABETH)* our Queen, and to all that are put in authority under her, that they may truly and impartially minister justice, to the punishment of wickedness and vice, and to the maintenance of thy true religion, and virtue.

Give grace, O heavenly Father, to all Bishops, Priests, and Deacons, especially to thy servant N. our bishop, that they may both by their life and doctrine set forth thy true and lively Word, and rightly and duly administer thy holy Sacraments.

Guide and prosper, we pray thee, those who are labouring for the spread of thy Gospel among the nations, and enlighten with thy Spirit all places of education and learning: that the whole world may be filled with the knowledge of thy truth.

And to all thy people give thy heavenly grace; and specially to this congregation here present; that, with meek heart and due reverence, they may hear, and receive thy holy Word; truly serving thee in holiness and righteousness all the days of their life.

And we most humbly beseech thee of thy goodness, O Lord, to comfort and succour all them, who in this transitory life are in trouble, sorrow, need, sickness, or any other adversity.

And we commend to thy gracious keeping, O Lord, all thy servants departed this life in thy faith and fear; beseeching thee to grant them everlasting light and peace.

And here we give thee most high praise and hearty thanks for all thy Saints, who have been the chosen vessels of thy grace, and lights of the world in their several generations; and we pray, that rejoicing in their fellowship and following their good examples, we may be partakers with them of thy heavenly kingdom:

Grant this, O Father, for Jesus Christ's sake, our only Mediator and Advocate; who liveth and reigneth with thee in the unity of the Holy Ghost, one God, world without end. **Amen.**

after the Sanctus-Benedictus:

ALL GLORY be to thee, Almighty God, our heavenly Father, for that thou of thy tender mercy didst give thine only Son Jesus Christ to suffer death upon the Cross for our redemption, who made there (by his one oblation of himself once offered) a full, perfect, and sufficient sacrifice, oblation, and satisfaction, for the sins of the whole world; and did institute, and in his holy Gospel command us to continue, a perpetual memory of that his precious death, until his coming again:

Who in the same night that he was betrayed, took Bread; and when he had given thanks, he brake it, and gave it to his disciples, saying, Take, eat, THIS IS MY BODY WHICH IS GIVEN FOR YOU; Do this in remembrance of me. Likewise after supper he took the Cup; and when he had given thanks, he gave it to them saying, Drink ye all of this, for THIS IS MY BLOOD OF THE NEW TESTAMENT, which is shed for you and for many for the remission of sins; Do this, as oft as ye shall drink it, in remembrance of me.

Wherefore O LORD and heavenly Father, we thy humble servants, having in remembrance the precious death and passion of thy dear Son, his mighty resurrection and glorious ascension, according to his holy institution, do celebrate, and set forth before thy divine Majesty, with these thy holy gifts, the memorial which he hath willed us to make, rendering unto thee most hearty thanks for the innumerable benefits which he hath procured for us.

Hear us, O merciful Father, we most humbly beseech thee; and with thy Holy and Life-giving Spirit vouchsafe to bless and sanctify both us and these thy gifts of Bread and Wine, that they may be unto us the Body and Blood of thy Son, our Saviour, Jesus Christ, to the end that we, receiving the same, may be strengthened and refreshed both in body and soul.

And we entirely desire thy fatherly goodness mercifully to accept this our sacrifice of praise and thanksgiving; most humbly beseeching thee to grant, that by the merits and death of the Son Jesus Christ, and through faith in his blood, we and all thy whole Church may obtain remission of our sins, and all other benefits of his passion.

And here we offer and present unto thee, O Lord, ourselves, our souls and bodies, to be a reasonable, holy, and living sacrifice unto thee: humbly beseeching thee, that all we, who are partakers of this Holy Communion, may be fulfilled with thy grace and heavenly benediction.

And although we be unworthy, through our manifold sins, to offer unto thee any sacrifice, yet we beseech thee to accept this our bounden duty and service; not weighing our merits, but pardoning our offences;

Through Jesus Christ our Lord, by whom, and with whom, in the unity of the Holy Ghost, all honour and glory be unto thee, O Father Almighty, world without end. **Amen.**

It is, however, more usual to use the 1928 form in its entirety if any part is used.

Before and After The Service

A form of Preparation

Celebrant: In the name of the Father, and of ✠ the Son, and of the Holy Ghost. Amen
I will go unto the altar of God:
Ministers: Even unto the God of my joy and gladness.
Cel: Give sentence with me, O God, and defend my cause against the ungodly people: O deliver me from the deceitful and wicked man.
M For thou art the God of my strength, why hast thou put me from thee: and why go I so heavily while the enemy oppresseth me?
C O send our thy light and thy truth, that they may lead me: and bring me unto thy holy hill, and to thy dwelling.
M And that I may go unto the Altar of God, even unto the God of my joy and gladness: and upon the harp will I give thanks unto thee, O God, my God.
C Why art thou so heavy, O my soul: and why art thou so disquieted within me?
M O put thy trust in God: for I will yet give him thanks, which is the help of my countenance, and my God.
C Glory be to the Father, and to the Son: and to the Holy Ghost.
M As it was in the beginning, is now, and ever shall be: world without end. Amen.
C I will go unto the altar of God.
M Even unto the God of my joy and gladness.

In Requiems and from Passion Sunday to Holy Saturday, the side-lined material is not said.

C   Our help is in the name ✠ of the Lord.

M   Who has made heaven and earth.

C *(bowing)*   I confess to almighty God, to blessed Mary ever Virgin, to blessed Michael the Archangel, to blessed John the Baptist, to the holy Apostles Peter and Paul, to all the Saints, and to you, my brothers and sisters that I have sinned exceedingly in thought, word and deed: *(he strikes his breast thrice, saying)* through my fault, through my fault, through my own most grievous fault; wherefore I pray blessed Mary ever Virgin, blessed Michael the Archangel, blessed John the Baptist, the holy Apostles Peter and Paul, all the Saints, and you, my brothers and sisters, to pray for me to the Lord our God.

M   May Almighty God have mercy upon thee, forgive thee all thy sins, and bring thee to everlasting life.

C *(standing up)* Amen.

M *(bowing)*   I confess to almighty God, to blessed Mary ever Virgin, to blessed Michael the Archangel, to blessed John the Baptist, to the holy Apostles Peter and Paul, to all the Saints, and to you, my father that I have sinned exceedingly in thought, word and deed: *(he strikes his breast thrice, saying)* through my fault, through my fault, through my own most grievous fault; wherefore I pray blessed Mary ever Virgin, blessed Michael the Archangel, blessed John the Baptist, the holy Apostles Peter and Paul, all the Saints, and you, my father, to pray for me to the Lord our God.

C   May Almighty God have mercy upon thee, forgive thee all thy sins, and bring thee to everlasting life.

M *(standing up)* Amen.

C   The Almighty and most merciful Lord grant unto us the pardon, ✠ absolution and remission of all our sins.

M   Amen.

C	Wilt thou not turn again, and quicken us, O Lord?
M	That thy people may rejoice in thee.
C	O Lord, shew thy mercy upon us.
M	And grant us thy salvation.
C	O Lord, hear my prayer.
M	And let my cry come unto thee.
C	The Lord be with you.
M	And with thy Spirit.
C	Let us pray.

Take away from us, we beseech thee, O Lord, all our iniquities: that we may be worthy to enter with pure minds into the Holy of holies, through Christ, out Lord.
M Amen.

The preceding form is sometimes said in the vestry before the liturgy, but is occasionally used at the altar before the service. After the liturgy in some churches the Angelus and Regina Coeli are used:

Angelus

The Angelus:

V: The Angel of the Lord brought tidings unto Mary.
R: And she conceived by the Holy Ghost.
Hail Mary, full of grace, the Lord is with thee: blessed art thou amongst women, and blessed is the fruit of thy womb, Jesus.
Holy Mary, Mother of God, pray for us sinners, now and at the hour of our death. Amen.

V: Behold the handmaid of the Lord.
R: Be it unto me according to thy word.
Hail Mary....

V: And the word was made flesh.
R: And dwelt among us.
Hail Mary....

V: Pray for us, O holy Mother of God.
R: That we may be made worthy of the promises of Christ.

We beseech thee, O Lord, pour thy grace into our hearts; that as we have known the Incarnation of thy Son Jesus Christ by the message of an angel, so by his Cross and Passion we may be brought unto the glory of his ✠ Resurrection. Through the same Christ our Lord. **Amen.**

Regina coeli (in Eastertide)

Joy to thee, O Queen of heaven, alleluia,
He whom thou was meet to bear, alleluia,
As he promised, hath arisen, alleluia,
Pour for us to God thy prayer, alleluia.

V: Rejoice and be glad, O Virgin Mary, alleluia.
R: For the Lord hath risen indeed, alleluia.

O God, who by the Resurrection of thy Son our Lord Jesus Christ hast given joy unto the world; grant we beseech thee that through the intercession of his Mother, the Virgin Mary, we may obtain the joys ✠ of life eternal. Through the same Christ our Lord. **Amen.**

From
The booke of Common praier noted
1550
by John Merbecke.

Because Merbecke used a plainsong stave and a type of notation derived from plainsong, with no barring, time indications or absolute/specified pitch, his settings are here edited for modern use. Time values have been shortened, but relative time lengths preserved. Merbecke was writing for the 1549 book and his order is followed. The Creed and Lord's Prayer are not given, being more often said. The Introit, Offertories, Preface, Canon & Post-Communions are all omitted, as either customarily sung to other tones (Preface),or no longer used or sung.
(Another setting commonly used is by Martin Shaw, and there are also quite a few alternatives, but Merbecke has nearly 400 years priority.).

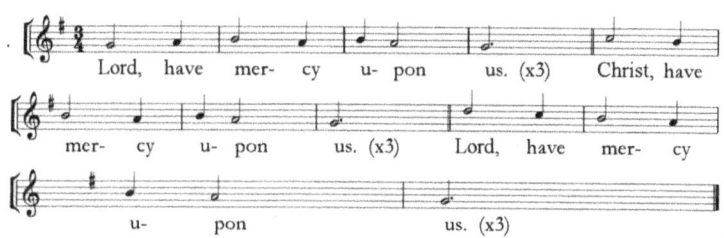

The following (not by, but derived from, Merbecke) exists in various forms: this version is editorial.

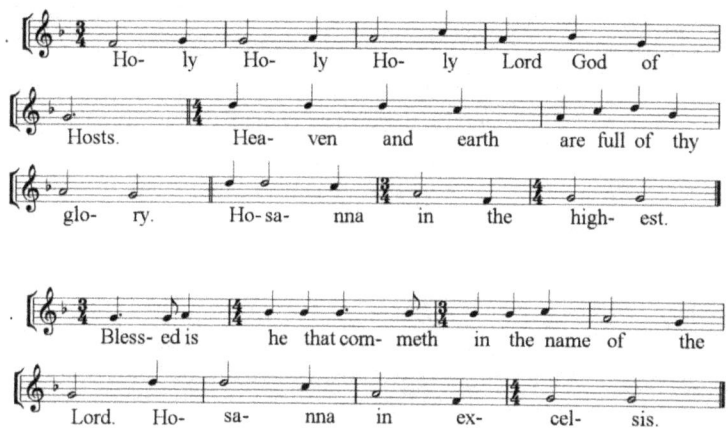
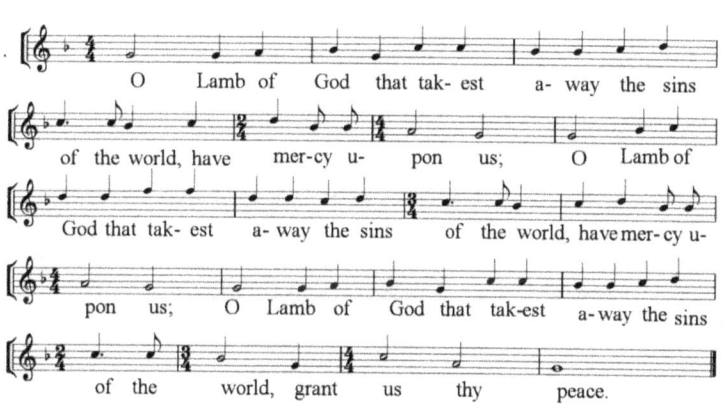

A Brief Commentary on the history & shape of Cranmer's eucharistic liturgy

Introductory

If you find yourself in a gathering of clerics, and mention the Book of Common Prayer, it is likely that someone will recount a yarn that goes much like this. "Some people in my church insisted that they wanted 1662, so I gave it to them, exactly as written. So nobody could receive communion who hadn't given notice the day before, we had the ten commandments, I read the exhortations, and then I made them repeat the prayers line by line, me saying a line and them saying it again[1]. They didn't ask again after that." If there is any truth in the yarn, and even if there is not, it shows, first, a breathtaking contempt for the cleric's parishioners, who just happen to be paying all or nearly all of his/her stipend, and, second, a literally wonderful ignorance of liturgy.

Many of the clergy, whose liturgical knowledge generally derives from what they were taught in theological college, gleaned from a handful of authors, but repetition of which makes them *soi disant* liturgical experts, think they know that Cranmer got it wrong, and that only the modern practices and rites have any authenticity, since they are, it is said, derived from the early Church.

---

[1] A practice described by Bishop Matthew Wren in 1636 as "that uncough and undecent custome of late taken up" and which he forbade. *Vide* Fincham *infra*.

To see, though, that it is more complex, consider the direction the priest faces: should s/he face the people across the altar or face in the same direction as them? Modern orthodoxy is that he/she must (*sic*) face the congregation across the altar.[2] The evidence from the early Church is actually that both practices are found, and have as much to do with the orientation of buildings and the design of altars as with anything else.[3,4] The early Church preference appears to have been for facing east whenever possible, with the westward position tolerated if it was unavoidable; the modern practice, in point of fact, is just that: modern.[5,6]

---

[2] Though the rubrics of the current Roman missal actually imply just the opposite. At "This is the Lamb of God" he is told to face the people, but for "May the body of Christ..." which follows immediately he is told to face the Altar; these instructions are redundant if he has been facing the people across the altar throughout, but make sense if he is using the eastward position. It was a misreading of the (ancient) requirement that it should be possible to walk around an altar – a requirement that the Tridentine form for consecrating churches illustrates (cf: Schulte AJ, *rev* O'Connell JB (1956) *Consecranda*, New York, Benziger Bros) – that gave Roman modernists their chance. The western-facing position was *never* intended by the Council or the Vatican, but had to be tolerated with a brave face as the misapprehension took hold and spread world-wide. The spirit of change after Vatican II was so strong that then explicitly ordering the eastward position was not an option the Vatican could take. It had to wait until John-Paul II before the beginnings of a return to the eastward position could be essayed.

[3] See Pocknee, C E (1963), *The Christian Altar*, Mowbray, Oxford for an older account, and Doig A (2008), *Liturgy and Architecture: From Early Church to the Middle Ages*, Ashgate, Aldershot for a modern and authoritative account of this question.

[4] Ask your parish priest for an opinion on the orders of Pope Vergilius concerning liturgical postures, and see if you get an answer.

[5] As some liturgical reformers admit. Cf: Baldovin J F (2009) *Reforming the Liturgy: A Response to the Critics*, Liturgical Press.

[6] NB: Jesus and the apostles did not sit round a table at the Last Supper; it is known that the Jewish custom was to recline, Roman-style, on major occasions.

In Cranmer's case, it needs to be made explicit that he didn't get it wrong: his liturgical shape is considered and deliberate. In him we are faced with someone seeking to find expression in the form of the eucharistic service for his particular beliefs, particularly those about the way Christ may be present in the elements of bread and wine, how far the eucharist is a sacrifice. His views are sometimes said to have developed over time, sometimes not.[7] Since Cranmer is the point of origin for all versions of the Book of Common Prayer, a brief outline of its history is in order.

Outline of Prayer Book History

Cranmer's first Prayer Book of 1549[8] is often regarded as a relatively straightforward translation of the Latin mass, but a comparison with the Use of Sarum will soon dispel that idea, and show that he was already shifting the emphasis of the service. Although he retained the traditional vestments[9], his changes to the canon of the mass substantially reduce the elements of offering and sacrifice.[10]

---

[7] See Jeanes G (2008) *Signs of God's Promise: Thomas Cranmer's Sacramental Theology and the Book of Common Prayer*, London & New York: T&T Clark, and McCulloch, D (1996), *Thomas Cranmer: A Life*, New Haven & London: Yale University Press, for contrasting views.

[8] Gibson B (int), (2008), *The First and Second Prayer Books of Edward VI*, Wildside is one of the few editions in print, though the 1938 Everyman's Library edition is standard.

[9] A letter from Bucer to Strasbourg makes it plain, however, that vestments were one element of what was intended as a temporary stage before a more radical reform. *(Epistolae Tigurinae p349f)*

[10] Already anticipated in his *Defence* of 1550. *(*see the edition of *Cranmer's works* by GE Duffield (1964)*)*.

His 1552 Prayer Book, however, was a far more radical revision[11], and it is from that text that all subsequent English editions of the Prayer Book derive. The structure of that revision is briefly discussed in the next section.

1553 saw Mary return to the throne, and the re-adoption of the Mass. How far her reign was welcomed by the people is a matter of debate, but her death in 1558, and the accession of Elizabeth I, makes that question purely academic. Whatever Elizabeth's own religious views were, and she was careful not to let these be known, her political sense told her that only a re-introduction of reformed religion was going to be acceptable, and in 1559 she re-issued the 1552 book.

Or, more accurately, the 1552 book with some subtle changes of wording, changes which gave a much more catholic flavour to the book. Amongst other changes, commemoration of the departed was re-introduced; at the administration the words "The Body of our Lord Jesus Christ..." replaced the bald "Eat this in remembrance that Christ died for thee, and feed on him in your heart..."; the prayer containing the Institution Narrative was called the "Prayer of Consecration"; the notorious `Black Rubric'[12] which denied any corporeal presence of Christ in the bread and wine was deleted;

---

[11] Gardiner in his *Explication and assertion of the Catholic faith* (*vide:* ed JA Muller (1933) *The Letters of Stephen Gardiner,* Cambridge) had provided a view of the 1549 book that was substantially consistent with catholic doctrine. Cranmer was determined that no such re-interpretation was going to be possible of the 1552 book.

[12] So called because it was printed in black, not in red as rubrics traditionally were.

and use of the traditional mass-vestments was ordered.[13,14]

In this form, the book continued in use down to the time of the civil war when it was completely displaced by puritan forms, chiefly the Directory. After the restoration of Charles II, the Savoy Conference, summoned to consider the form of book that should be ordered, rejected almost every major suggestion made, and re-adopted the 1559 book, but with numerous minor verbal changes, intended to throw a sop or two to the Puritans. The 1552 and 1559 words of administration were combined, and a re-worded 'black rubric' was re-instated, though the rule concerning vestments and the term 'Prayer of Consecration' were retained. The word 'priest' replaced 'minister' at the absolution. The combination meant that the book was capable of different interpretations, perhaps or definitely deliberately. This, the 1662 book, remains unchanged down to the present day.[15]

---

[13] Booty, J E ed (1976, 2nd ed 2005), *The Book of Common Prayer 1559, The Elizabethan Prayer Book*, University of Virginia Press, Charlottesville and London includes the full book, together with a very useful history and notes, which are indispensable to anyone interested in the history of the Prayer Book

[14] However, ordering the Anglican clergy to do something, and actually getting them to do it, were, then as now, two very different things. Although the traditional vestments were certainly ordered, implicitly if not explicitly, there is no evidence that they were used anywhere, even in the Queen's own chapel; surplices, sometimes with copes, were as far as most of the clergy were prepared to go. For two modern parallels, how many clergy are willing to follow the common law and allow the use of their Church for the 1662 service of burial to be said for any parishioner, even though should they refuse then the next of kin or executor can requisition the Church at any reasonable hour and read the 1662 service him/herself; and how many clergy flout the plain law that requires them to baptize any child of a parishioner if requested?

[15] Cardwell, E (1849) *A History of Conferences and other Proceedings connected with the revision of the Book of Common Prayer from the Year 1558 to the Year 1690*, Oxford,

After an abortive attempt later in the century to move the book in a more protestant direction, the form then ossified. A revision proposed in 1879 was rejected by parliament. Anglo-Catholics and High Churchmen then introduced various changes, and brought legal confusion with them, provoking the Privy Council into a very questionable judgement on the Ornaments Rubric which held that despite what the 1662 book says, the 'Advertisements' issued by Archbishop Parker in 1566 took priority, and the surplice rather than the vestments must be used, but permitting copes in cathedrals and collegiate establishments.

Outside England, in 1764 a revised book was introduced in Scotland, in 1789 an American version was instituted which was revised several times and particularly in 1892, in 1877 an Irish Prayer Book was established, and in 1912 the Scottish Prayer Book was revised. The American Prayer Book is of considerable importance, since its contents formed the basis of the 1928 attempted revision of the English Book.

The story of the 1928 attempt at revision is too long to be summarised here, but it can be said that a quite limited revision, intended to allow the more moderate changes that clergy had introduced but retaining Cranmer's language, though altering the shape to something closer to catholic usage, passed through the Convocations of Canterbury and York, and the House of Lords, to be rejected by the House of Commons.

(reprinted Nabu), is an excellent sourcebook for the various revisions, particularly for the Savoy Conference.

Those updated versions that appeared outside England, most particularly the American book, just as Cranmer had used 1549 to create 1552, used 1559 and 1549 to create a fairly conservative revision that met changing needs, including a marked shift in theology away from Cranmer's view of the real presence, and a consequent re-shaping of the material, deliberately abandoning Cranmer's shape. The result was that use of the BCP outside England in the 20th Century was more widespread outside England than in it.

If the 1928 revision had been allowed, it is almost certain that a form of the Book of Common Prayer would have stayed in use, though it might well have required some further revision in the light of the liturgical movement of the 1960's. It may or may not be seen as ironic that by insisting on keeping the Prayer Book unchanged, the House of Commons consigned it, in the long run, to virtual insignificance as a vehicle for worship in the Church of England. [16]

---

[16] Procter, F; Frere, W H (1965), *A New History of the Book of Common Prayer*, St. Martin's Press, is the standard history of the Book of Common Prayer. Booty *op cit* is valuable for the area it covers, while MacCulloch *op cit* contains indispensable material on 1549 & 1552. Hefling, C.; C. Shattuck, *Eds* (2006). *The Oxford Guide to The Book of Common Prayer: A Worldwide Survey*. Oxford: Oxford University Press, is also of some (surprisingly rather limited) use, though as with all compilations the standard of the different articles is very varied; it should be noted that over half the work deals with the modern liturgies rather than the BCP itself. An older book, Harford G. & Stevenson M, (1912) *The Prayer Book Dictionary*, London: Pitman, is a mine of background information and should not be overlooked.

Outline of Cranmer's liturgical shape

It has been mentioned above that it is unclear how far Cranmer's theological opinions developed over time. What is clear is that in the 1552 book he is expressing deeply protestant opinions, yet ones which cannot readily be identified with those of Calvin, Zwingli, Oecolampadius, Peter Martyr or any of the major continental reformers.

Regarding the presence of Christ in the eucharist, Cranmer certainly denied any element of corporeal presence of the body and blood of Christ in the bread and wine: there was no transubstantiation or anything like it. The bread and wine were, in themselves, unchanged. On the other hand, he would not accept that the Lord's supper was simply a reminder or sign of Christ's presence; he insisted that in some way Christ was really present. Nor would he accept that Christ was present only in those who received the bread and wine; in some way Christ was present in the whole sacrament.
I do not think that there is anywhere any really straightforward account of what Cranmer believed for the simple reason that he didn't have a straightforward belief. Logically, he was protestant; emotionally, he still had a strong catholic strand of devotion to Christ.[17] One image, however, that he used, and which can be seen to have affected his liturgy, was that Christ was present in the sacrament in the same way he was present in his Word. He is really present in His Words, but not to be identified in any way with the sounds or signs that

---

[17] My purpose here is purely to discuss Cranmer's liturgical shape; see Jeanes and McCulloch, *ops cit*, for Cranmer's theological views.

make up words; similarly His Body and Blood were truly present in the communion, but are not to be identified with any particular part of the rite.

The link in his mind between Christ's Words and Sacraments is fundamental to his thinking and to his liturgy. He wanted to bring them into the closest possible relation to each other.

So he took a startlingly radical step. Prior to him, the Mass had had an offertory, a long prayer of consecration which included our Lord's words of institution, a breaking of the bread during the Agnus Dei, and, after preparatory prayers, finally the communion, so that each of the things Christ did and said is present, but as part of a stretched-out and longer sequence. Cranmer, on the other hand, made word and act into a single conjoined whole, based on our Lord's words. As the priest says "He took bread", he takes the bread; as he says "he broke it", he breaks it; when he says of the cup "Drink this", the wine is drunk. To make this conception work, he had to postpone the eating of the bread a few moments, so that the eating of the bread and drinking of the wine could occur together, but otherwise what Christ did is re-enacted at the precise moment that the relevant word or act of Christ is mentioned in the account of the institution.[18]

Allow that premise, and all else follows. Of the Lord's Prayer, Christ had said that when we pray, it was what we were to say, so all rites link it to the prayer of

---

[18] The giving thanks is going on continuously from the Preface onwards, but reaches its high point in the prayer that contains our Lord's words.

consecration and to the communion. Cranmer places it immediately next to the communion because the communion and the saying of the Lord's Prayer are equally acts of obedience.

The material of oblation (offering) in all rites follows the words of institution, and so it does in Cranmer's order. It is not to be seen as being, in 1552 and its *sequelae*, a post-communion prayer:- it is a continuation of the consecratory material which has included both word and action. Put another way, the communion occurs in the middle of *one* prayer that includes both the account of the institution and also the oblation[19]. (The post-communion thanksgiving he gives as an alternative, has, on examination, material that functions in ways similar to an oblation of the self.)

Now the other material all falls into place, and its order becomes entirely logical.

The prayer of humble access is the immediate preparation for communion, so it must go into the first available space before the communion, which is after the Sanctus.

Cranmer knew from his study of the ancient liturgies that the Benedictus is a later accretion, so he omitted it, leaving the Sanctus to stand alone after the Preface, with the Hosanna in excelsis translated into an English form.

---

[19] Although Cranmer changes the material of the oblation substantially, this is, nonetheless the equivalent passage to that in older rites.

The Preface, Cranmer reduced to its essential parts – an ascription of praise joined with that of heaven -, using additional material only on the greatest feasts.

The confession of the people, in the western rites, came at that time shortly before communion, and so Cranmer finds it an equivalent place – just before the sequence that is going to lead to the communion. To diminish any impression that the absolution was a priestly act[20], he inserted the comfortable words.

The prayer for the Church Militant is the intercessory material of the Canon of the Mass, which, as Cranmer also knew, was placed in different places in different liturgies. For his purposes, it makes most sense to place it immediately after the Offertory. What it most emphatically is not, is a misplaced version of the modern prayers of the people; no Western rite had had such an element for some centuries, and the Eastern rites had transformed them into the litanies that are such a feature of the liturgies of St John Chrysostom and Basil still used by the Orthodox. Prayers of the people are a modern re-invention, and Cranmer can

---

[20] Interestingly, the modern Roman rite has done exactly the same thing: the Latin is "Misereatur nostri omnipotens Deus dimissis peccatis nostris, perducat nos ad vitam aeternam." which should be translated as "May almighty God have mercy on us, and, forgiving us our sins {or 'with our sins forgiven'}, lead us to eternal life.". This is then followed by a prayer for that mercy, in the Kyries. The versions of confession that are normally used, are, in the Latin, occasional alternatives to be used when particularly appropriate, and are placed in an appendix. In the liturgy likely to be used by Anglicans who accept the Pope's 2010 offer to join an ordinariate, the Comfortable Words are retained after an amended absolution.
The Stuart and Caroline bishops were clear that, despite the extra wording, it was a priestly absolution (*Vide* Fincham *infra*).

hardly be blamed for not inventing them when he knew that every liturgy had given them up.

So, the shape of Cranmer's equivalent of the Roman Canon starts at the offertory and continues, though apparently split into parts, in a logical sequence right through to the prayer of oblation. It is a single liturgical piece devised to unite Christ's eucharistic Words and Acts as they had, after all, been united at the Last Supper.

The position of the Gloria at the end of the service now makes sense: it is the act of praise that provides thanksgiving for communion.[21]

Cranmer has closely linked Word and Sacrament; but what he has also done – and for this is he is given far too little credit – is keep a continuity with the contents of the Mass. The Canon, true, is broken up, and its emphasis much changed, but most of its parts are still present. It lacks an explicit *anamnesis*[22], and the *epiclesis*[23] which had appeared in 1549 has disappeared again – but that had gone from the Roman Mass too, long before. Otherwise one can trace the divers parts of the Roman Canon in one or other place in Cranmer's text. Here Cranmer differs from Lutheran and Calvinist rites, for both of those liturgical families, while not totally losing

---

[21] Which is why it should never be omitted, even in Lent or Advent.

[22] The passage where the priest specifically makes remembrance of the work of Christ, particularly His passion and resurrection. It is certainly arguable, however, that the introduction to the Prayer of Consecration serves as an anamnesis.

[23] The prayer that God the Father will send the Holy Spirit to consecrate the bread and wine into Christ's Body and Blood.

all signs of the Roman exemplar, jettison most of the Canon altogether, and so have to be regarded as breaking the basic linkage with the Mass. The Preface and the Words of Institution are the only parts preserved in some protestant rites.

This means that however much one may see Cranmer as a protestant thinker, in his liturgy, even in 1552, he is a reformer not a radical remaker, and it makes his work *sui generis*. It is not too much to say that Cranmer is the only reformation figure who can be regarded as producing a rite that reforms the Roman source, but does not lose contact with it. That was the avowed aim of at least the early reformers – to reform and purify the Roman Mass, taking it back to something closer to apostolic origins. Liturgically, only Cranmer meets that aim. That he did so makes possible the classic Anglican identity that can hold protestants and catholics together in one communion.[24]

It is vital, therefore, to recognise that while Cranmer's liturgical shape was radical, by itself it is perfectly capable of a catholic understanding: the union of Word and Sacrament is a classic and orthodox theme, and as a reform of *shape* is actually an attractive idea when given appropriate wording. Only with 1552 is an unavoidably protestant result achieved. 1559 and 1662 each will take

---

[24] Recently in a conversation, someone said to me that Vatican II had had more negative implications for Anglicans than for Roman Catholics; inasmuch as the *zeitgeist* pushed the Prayer Book out of collective Anglican consciousness, in the long run it made schisms and party hostility within the C of E far more extreme – the Prayer Book was part of the mortar between the Anglican bricks (in all sorts of ways...).

both catholic and protestant interpretations, as already stated.

The Exhortations

It remains to deal with the lengthy exhortations which are, in the 1662 book, all printed before the invitation to confession. Their history is not exactly straightforward, which is why it is worth treating them separately from the rest of Cranmer's material.

They appear at first sight to be intrusive texts, interrupting the flow of the service and destroying much of the shape. On closer inspection, they don't have that effect, partly because of how they are to be used, and partly on how often.

In 1548, an english rite for receiving communion was published. It contained a lengthy exhortation to the people, shortly before they were to receive.[25] Here, though the rite is undoubtedly Protestant in direction, and aims to drive home the importance of what the communicants are about to do, it makes liturgical sense in terms of the shape, being followed by an invitation for the sinful to withdraw, then confession and absolution[26], and the prayer of humble access. It was when attempts were made to include this exhortation in the new Prayer Books that problems arose: there is no place where the exhortation does not stick out like a sore thumb, for it belongs best close to the communion, but the changes of 1552, and Cranmer's union of Word

---

[25] See Maskell, *op. cit.*
[26] The absolution is surprisingly sacerdotal in tone.

and Sacrament, make this impossible. Actually, if its use were to be regarded as essential, shifting it to the very beginning of the service would make most sense, by turning it into a commentary on the importance of the service that is about to occur[27].

In the 1549 book, there are two exhortations. The first is directed to be used if the sermon does not itself in some way exhort the people to receive the sacrament worthily[28]. It is then said that the exhortation is, in places where there is daily communion, sufficiently used if it is said once a month, and that in parish churches it need not be said on week-days. No frequency of use in parish churches is prescribed. The second is for use to the parishioners in general when notice is given of a forthcoming communion - if the priest finds the people are negligent in attending communion. That indicates that the second exhortation can, in practice, only have been used at a service where there was no communion. The result is that in the majority of communion services there would have been no exhortation.

In the 1552 book, the exhortations number three, and are moved to their present place after the prayer for the church militant. However, the first is to be used at "certain times" when the priest sees the people negligent to come to communion, while the second is to be used "some tyme" at the discretion of the minister. As with the first exhortation of 1549, these two were

---

[27] Though I am not advocating using the exhortations, to have an occasional reminder of the need for serious preparation for communion and of the awesomeness of that act would be both wise and helpful in this age of weekly communion.
[28] And so is the equivalent of the third exhortation of later rites.

therefore not used if there were actually a communion. The rubric for the third is "then shall the priest say this exhortation", but it is not explicit as to when "then" is. It may be for use before every confession, or after the first exhortation, or even after the second. Its language and emphasis are congruent with those of the first two, which is why the confusion as to "then" matters: the congruency of language make the third exhortation belong most naturally in the same place as the other two. On the other hand, it also fits well with continental and puritan usage, where long exhortations before communion were a feature of the service, and it is known that Cranmer had been put under much pressure by continental reformers. That would place it before the confession when the service includes communion, and this is certainly the most probable intended place. Whichever position was intended, there are indications that many clergy ignored it. As we shall see, there is considerable likelihood that it was only the puritans who used it, where it was used at all. Given that the 1552 book had only a year's use, and met with resistance, it is not really possible to decide whether it ever found general use.

In the 1559 book, the rubrics are repeated from the 1552 book, but any doubt about how the first two exhortations were used is settled for us by the Canons (church laws) issued in 1603/4. Canon 22 makes it explicit that notice of the Communion is to be given the week before, during Morning Prayer.[29] Those Canons

---

[29] An examination of the Visitation records, when Archdeacons and Bishops held (and hold) inspections of parishes, shows their concerns quite plainly, and consequently gives a picture of what was going on in parishes. While there is

retained their force even after the 1662 book – in fact, right through to the 1970's.

Accordingly, whatever ambiguities there may be in the rubrics in the Prayer Book, the Canons make plain that it is only the third exhortation that could have been used during an actual communion service itself (as opposed to a partial service with no actual communion). The Canons also make clear that there was a strong desire to exclude puritanism from having any effect on the church. Canon 21 insists on the use of the words of institution, and that the priest must receive the communion himself whenever he takes the service.

Given the change in the political and religious climate, it is difficult to see that the bishops appointed by Elizabeth would have been zealous in requiring the use of the third exhortation. We know that communion had begun to be celebrated but seldom, and that ensuring that it was celebrated with some regularity and sufficient decency was the main priority. Those visitation records that survive do not support the idea that the bishops regularly enquired whether the exhortation was used, and the probability is that the rubrics were given a very loose interpretation. If so, it is likely that the exhortations were used seldom, if at all, in mainstream, as opposed to puritan, churches.[30]

---

frequent emphasis on notice of communion being given, it is the Canon rather than the rubric which is predominantly cited, with Bishop Matthew Wren (1636) being exceptional in placing the notice to be given using the first two exhortations after the Prayer for the Church Militant – but he is explicit that no actual communion is to follow. *Cf* Fincham *infra*.

[30]. The Visitation records show little interest in the exhortations. A few bishops stress the importance of advertising the availability of the clergy to help quiet the conscience, while slightly more are concerned that the

This impression is strengthened by the fact that in the 1662 book one of the changes from 1559 was to strengthen the rubric for the third exhortation. It now reads that the priest "shall" say it at the time of communion, a change that is plain evidence that the exhortation had not attained to general use while the 1559 book was in force.

This new insistence on its use should not be taken at face value. The changes made by the Savoy Conference which preceded the issuing of the 1662 book were concessions to the puritan party to make it easier for them to return to being part of the Church of England and to having a fixed book at all, rather than being allowed free prayer as their ministers had been used to during the Cromwellian period. We have already seen that 1662 reintroduces the 'Black Rubric', yet it is fairly clear that for the clergy of the broad and high churches that was quietly overlooked, not least because the rest of the service is expressed in terms substantially inconsistent with the black rubric. It is likely that being ignored was the general fate of the exhortation, too. We cannot be certain, but the balance of probability must be that it never entered widespread use in the reformation and the immediate post-reformation

---

Absolutions, both in the Communion and the Offices, are performed as absolutions and not general declarations. As already noted, Bishop Wren requires the use of the first two exhortations in the absence of a communion, but only Bishop Richard Montagu (1638) mentions the third exhortation at all, though he does require it to be said immediately prior to the confession. (See: Frere W.H. (reprint 2010) *Visitation Articles and Injunctions of the Period of the Reformation: 1536-1558*, BiblioBazaar; and: Fincham K ed (1998) *Visitation Articles and Injunctions of the Early Stuart Church*, 2 volumes, Boydell).

period. Admittedly, if the third exhortation was widely used, the logic of Cranmer's shape would be partly obscured, though by no means lost. It is certain that the puritans wanted to go much further than Cranmer and had little regard for his work. It is equally evident that that was not the sentiment of the mainstream clergy.

Although it is again impossible to be certain, the period in which it is probable that the third exhortation did become widely used, and indeed an invariable part of the service, is what has been called the "long eighteenth century" – late 1600's to mid 1800's – when the doctrinal concerns of the clergy had shifted, and conformity was paramount.[31]

For the nineteenth century, from the period after the Tractarian movement took hold there are enough surviving Altar books in which the third exhortation is either omitted altogether or else printed so as to be conveniently overlooked to make it plain that the exhortation was starting to be deliberately ignored by many clergy. Since there is in Tractarian and Anglo-Catholic little if any discussion or advocacy of the omission, the inference that the omission predated the Tractarian movement is a reasonable one. At some point the Broad Church also gave up its use, but this is more difficult to date[32].

---

[31] See Jacob W.M. (2007), *The Clerical Profession in the Long Eighteenth Century 1680-1840*, Oxford, OUP.
[32] Taylor N (1993), *For Services Rendered*, Cambridge: The Lutterworth Press, makes the very reasonable suggestion that use of the exhortations died out once weekly communion became the norm.

If we accept the probability that the exhortations were not generally used in the Reformation period, then clergy who conduct "reconstructions" of the "original" Prayer Book Service have no need to include the third exhortation – and are precluded from including the first two.[33]

The Uses – and Usage

"Now from hēcefurth, all the whole realme shall haue but one use." With those words, the Preface to the 1549 Book called time on the uses of Salisbury, Hereford, Bangor, York, Lincoln and all the other manifold ways of saying and singing the services in England; - except that it couldn't possibly achieve that in practice. There was a problem with 1549, in that it simply didn't describe what was to be done in enough detail for the clergy to know what was required of them. Here are some examples: 1549 stipulates an Introit, but has two places for it to be sung, before and after the Our Father; at the Collect, it tells the priest to face the people for "The Lorde be with you.", but doesn't tell him to turn back, so which way should he face for the prayers?; it says the Epistle shall be read "in a place assigned" but doesn't say what that is; it doesn't say where the Gospel shall be read, where the priest begins the Creed, where the Offertory sentences should be said, etc, etc. Some of these are easy to solve, but others

---

[33] Please note that I am not arguing that the exhortations were *never* used, but rather that they were rare. Single instances of their use are not therefore probative against the view expressed here. It would require showing that more churches used them than not, and such evidence does not appear to exist.

only make any sense if you already know the answer.[34] It was inevitable, therefore, that people would adapt the instructions to fit what they were already used to. The Bishops' Visitation records indicate that the Bishops weren't much concerned about how such things were done – it was enough to get the book used, and that decently, at all.

The short-lived Book of 1552 simplified the ritual substantially, but Mary brought back the Mass, and therefore the old Uses.

When Elizabeth re-introduced the Prayer Book in 1559, there was some loosening of rubrics, and we know that there was great variation in how people used the Book. Some made it as near-Puritan as they could, while others clung to as many of the old ways as they could. Again, it is clear from the Visitation records that the Bishops concerned themselves with essentials and let a great deal of variation (towards which, in any case, they themselves had very different outlooks) go unchallenged.

Although over time the predominant anti-Catholic feeling grew and worship became slowly but surely

---

[34] Maskell W. (1882), *The ancient Liturgy of the Church of England According to the uses of Sarum York Hereford and Bangor and the Roman Liturgy arranged in parallel columns with preface and notes,* Oxford: Clarendon Press, is a useful source for comparing Uses, but suffers from Maskell only using one missal for each Use, with that for Bangor being of perhaps questionable attribution, and therefore ignores historical developments and differences between sources. Even so, it is a good starting point. For Sarum, there are many secondary sources that are patchy, but the works of Frere (too numerous to list) are of undoubted value. Relevant volumes from *The Henry Bradshaw Society*, now published by Boydell, are also pertinent.

more overtly Protestant, religious practice is generally inherently conservative: people *like* doing what they are used to. So while the grand ceremonies of the old Uses certainly disappeared, equally certainly, little fragments will have remained in the ways things were done. It's also worth bearing in mind that to talk of the Uses of Salisbury, York, etc can obscure first, that there were other famed Uses that remained purely local, such as the London Use, and secondly, the fact that virtually every church will have had its own peculiarities, not least because of resources: if your parish has only two chasubles, you can't follow an elaborate colour scheme, while if your parish has a shrine to Saint X but your neighbour has one to Saint Y, then the observance of their days will vary (and though such things were later banned and destroyed, we have evidence that the laity, at least, found ways of holding on to their old ways). It took a very long time for the remains of Catholic usage and Use to fade and disappear, if they ever totally did.

Given that no-one in the Church of England now worships in the near-Calvinist style which the reformers eventually made the norm (though it took into the 18th century to achieve it), and that a richer liturgy is universal, it seems not merely reasonable but laudable to celebrate local heritage.

That said, to reconstruct the Uses varies in possibility: Bangor and York are near impossible because the service books have very little detail in the rubrics, whereas Sarum is detailed and precise to the point of absurdity and Hereford is detailed, but not prolix. The scribes seem have to have taken much for granted as likely to be already known, and only to have written the essential or unusual rubrics. Even so, they still manage to cause confusion. At York there were definitely two lavabos at the Offertory, but neither of the two positions given seems particularly likely, and there must be some lingering doubt over the correctness of the rubrics. Celebrating a full service on the basis of the old books is only really worth doing as a (in some cases hypothetical) historical reconstruction.

What discussion of the Uses most illustrates is that there are a range of additional decisions that have to be made before the Book of Common Prayer can be used. The alternatives that this present little book calls attention to are testimony enough to that; and, consequently, testimony to the fact that modern Uses have developed in great number. The work of Percy Dearmer lies behind many to a greater or lesser extent, but it has to be said that he was perhaps not always entirely straightforward in his use of sources. The quirks of local Church architecture, the quiddities of Anglican churchmanship and the greater quirkiness of clergy over approximately the last century and a half accounts for much of the variation. Although, therefore, we have to be clear that the idea of there being a single correct way of celebrating 1662 is not sustainable, with care and a little historical awareness it is possible to create a local style which is dignified, suits our predilections and yet effectively respects the BCP rubrics. Once that much is done, the text, provided the celebrant speaks it with measured clarity, will ever demonstrate the beautiful features of the rite.

That said, three observations[35] are perhaps in order. The BCP rubrics specify the priest commencing the service standing at the Altar and remaining there until at least after the Collect; this makes the modern use of a President's Chair inappropriate. The rubrics also specify the priest's turning to the people at various points, which argues against a westward-facing celebration. Finally, despite the undoubted beauty of a well-made surplice[36], the Ornaments Rubric, properly understood, does require vestments[37].

Irreversible changes do occur: for example, in Cranmer's day there would have been no hymns as we understand them, but we can hardly imagine a sung service without them; altars will not be orientated north-south again any time soon, and so on. It is a testament to how well Cranmer and the Elizabethan and Caroline revisers did their respective tasks that in the intervening centuries each age has been able to make this service their own, and that that will continue to be the case for the indefinite future.

Conclusion

I have tried, in this brief piece, to explain that Cranmer certainly didn't "get it wrong". Actually he wrote a brilliantly innovative reformed liturgy that joined the

---

[35] NB: observations, not prescriptions.
[36] Preferably full-length, Old English style, worn without stole, scarf or hood. It should go without saying also that cottas and lace-decorated albs are out of place.
[37] In the design of which, incidentally, we are not bound by any rule to the Roman four-colour pattern; pre-Reformation usage included many other colours.

Word and the Sacrament together, regaining consistency of the liturgy with the biblical sources. Once one sees his aim, then his sequence is completely logical,[38] and one can appreciate the liturgical, as well as linguistic, brilliance demonstrated by Cranmer in his work.

That sequence is expressed in language which was originally devised, in 1549, for a rather different rite. The 1559 and 1662 alterations of his 1552 rite, which is the last one for which he is actually responsible, made possible a wider range of understandings of the way Christ is present and of the sacrificial aspect of the rite.

It is interesting that those changes don't invalidate the shape of his liturgy or of his conjoining Word and Sacrament as closely as he did. In fact, they leave us, in the 1662 book, with a service that is both reformed and catholic, which is why it served the Church of England so well for so long, and one reason why it deserves to be cherished and enjoyed still.

Alec McGuire

---

[38] It also means that **nothing** should be inserted into the service at the time of Communion: neither the Agnus Dei nor post-communion hymns nor organ music are appropriate, since the insertion of any of them entirely destroys the shape of the liturgy, by making the oblation into a post-communion. One can, just about, contend for the Agnus Dei being understood in a way similar to the modern "Let us proclaim the mystery of faith" acclamations, but such an argument smacks of unconvincing *post hoc* pragmatism; the Cranmerian shape is still being heavily deformed. Anyway, as an atheist friend of mine points out periodically, if communion is such a transcendently important act, why do you have music that whiles away the time? If people are having communion in the Body and Blood of Christ, how can it possibly be appropriate for anything else to be happening? If actions speak louder than words, then you are saying either that Christ isn't present or that you'd like to listen to tunes instead. In thirty years I've never been able to think of a riposte to his logic.

www.ingramcontent.com/pod-product-compliance
Lightning Source LLC
Chambersburg PA
CBHW051714040426

42446CB00008B/886